A DROP OF BLOOD

BY *Paul Showers*
illustrated by Don Madden

THOMAS Y. CROWELL COMPANY NEW YORK

There is blood everywhere inside your body.

When you cut yourself, you make a hole in your skin.

Blood leaks out through the hole.

If the cut is small, it soon stops bleeding.

Oh, there's blood in your arms and your legs,
There's blood in your fingers and toes,
     And once in awhile
     When a game gets too rough,
You'll find that there's blood in your nose.

You don't have to cut yourself—
    or bump yourself—
    to find out where your blood is.
You can *see* where it is.

You can look at your blood with a flashlight.

Go into a room tonight and shut the door.
Turn on the flashlight in the dark.
Hold your fingers over the light.
What color are they?

Look in the mirror in the dark.
Hold the flashlight behind your ear.
What color is your ear?
Put the flashlight in your mouth.
What color are your cheeks?
The blood in your fingers and your ear and your
  cheeks makes them look red.

Blood is red because it is full of tiny red cells.
They are VERY tiny.
There are hundreds—
    and thousands—
        and millions—
            of them in a single drop of blood.

Red cells are too small to see with your eye.
You have to look at them under a microscope.

Then the red cells look like this—

round and flat,
thin in the middle,
thick around the edge—
something like tiny doughnuts without any holes.

The blood is always moving inside your body.
It moves through little tubes.
It moves out to the tips of your fingers.
It moves up to your head and down to your toes.
Wherever your blood goes, the red cells go with it.

The red cells carry oxygen.

Oxygen is part of the air you breathe.

You cannot see oxygen, but you cannot live without
it.

Your body has to have oxygen every minute.

You breathe oxygen into your lungs.

The red cells in your blood take the oxygen from
your lungs.

Red cells carry the oxygen to every part of your
body.

They carry oxygen to your muscles—
    to your bones—
      your brain—
        your stomach—
          your heart.

Your body needs food as well as oxygen.
It uses oxygen and food to make you warm and to
  keep you strong.

muscles

bones

brain

heart

stomach

When you eat, the food goes down to your stomach
and your intestines.
There the food is changed into a fluid.
The fluid moves from your intestines into your blood.
You cannot see the food any more, even under a
microscope.
But it is in your blood. So is the oxygen that the
red cells are carrying.

Your blood takes the food to every part of your
body.
It takes food to your bones to make them grow,
to your muscles to make them strong,
to your fingers and your toes—
even to your brain.

There are white cells in your blood, too.
They are bigger than red cells.
Your blood has fewer white cells than red cells.
But there are thousands of white cells in one drop
   of blood.

White cells protect you against disease germs.
A white cell wraps itself around a germ and covers
   it up.
When the germ is trapped inside the white cell, it
   cannot harm you.

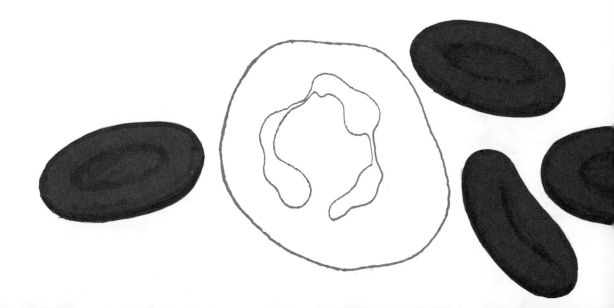

Some things in your blood are smaller than the
white cells—even smaller than the red cells.
They have no color.
They are flat and round, like little plates.
They are called PLATElets.

When you cut your skin, blood runs out.
Platelets help stop the bleeding.
They help to make tiny threads in your blood.
These threads are called fibrin.

The fibrin threads make a net across the cut.
Red cells and white cells are caught in the net.
Soon the net becomes thick with red and white cells.
The blood cannot flow through it.
The bleeding stops.
The net hardens and becomes a scab.
New skin grows under the scab, and closes the cut.

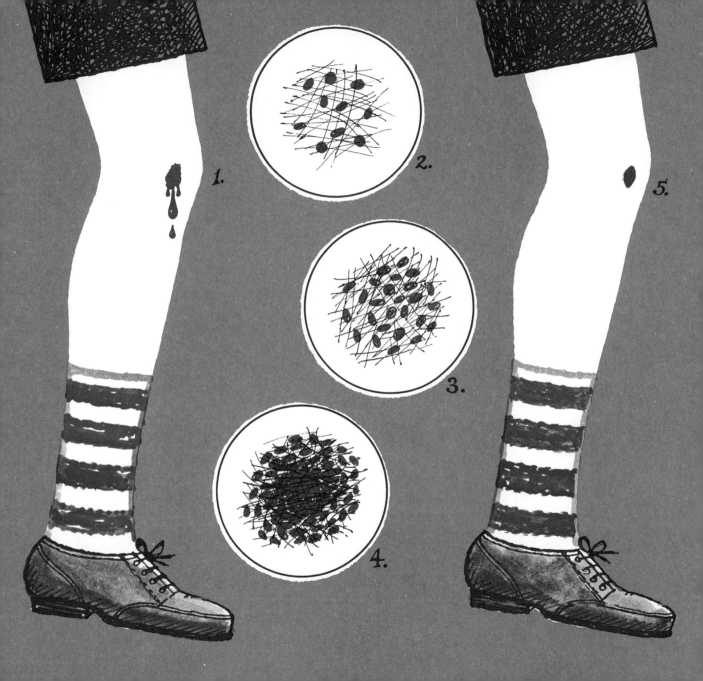

Little people do not need much blood.

Cathy is one year old. She weighs twenty-four
pounds.

She has about one and a half pints of blood in her
body.

That is less than one quart.

Big people need more blood.
Russell is eleven years old.
He weighs eighty-eight pounds.
He has about five and a half
    pints of blood in his body.

That is a little less than three
    quarts.

Bill is six feet tall. He weighs 180 pounds.

He has about eleven pints of blood.

Eleven pints are the same as five and a half quarts.

Red cells do not last forever.
They wear out.
White cells and platelets wear out, too.
But your body makes new ones all the time.
Every day it makes new red and white cells and new
   platelets.

When you cut yourself, you lose some blood.
You lose red cells and white cells. You lose platelets.
But that doesn't matter.
Your body has plenty of new ones to take their place.
It keeps making new ones all the time.

Sometimes I cut my finger,
  Sometimes I scrape my knee.
Sometimes a drop or two of blood
  Comes dripping out of me.

That means I lose some platelets,
  Some white cells and some red;
I lose them by the millions
  In every drop I shed.

But I don't get excited
  About my bleeding skin—
For all the blood that oozes OUT
  There's plenty more that's IN.

ABOUT THE AUTHOR

Paul Showers is a New York newspaperman and writer of more than a dozen books for children. He first became interested in making books for young readers after watching his own children struggle with the "See, Sally, see" books of the 1950's ("television's greatest boon," he calls them). His own books, most of them in the Let's-Read-and-Find-Out series, have thoroughly proved that children's books can be both lively and worth while.

Mr. Showers began newspaper work on the Detroit *Free Press*. Then came the New York *Herald Tribune*, a brief stint on the New York *Sunday Mirror* and, for the past twenty-five years, the Sunday *New York Times*. Mr. Showers was born in Sunnyside, Washington, and has an A.B. degree from the University of Michigan.

ABOUT THE ARTIST

Don Madden attended the Philadelphia Museum College of Art on a full scholarship. Following graduation he became a member of the faculty for two years as an instructor in experimental drawing and design. The recipient of gold and silver medals at the Philadelphia Art Director's Club exhibitions, Mr. Madden's work has been selected for reproduction in the New York Art Director's Annual and in the international advertising art publication, *Graphis*, and has been included in the overseas traveling art exhibits of the United States Information Agency. He has illustrated articles for *Seventeen, Good Housekeeping, Harper's Bazaar*, and *Parents' Magazine*. Mr. Madden lives in New York City with his family.